Foreword

The material for this book, like all the books in the Homeschool Parents' How-To Series, first appeared as a seminar presented at homeschool conventions in my home state of Texas.

Over and over parents responded enthusiastically and asked me to make the material available in book form so they could refer back to the information through the course of their homeschool journey.

I'm happy to do that.

Because the material was designed for presentation in a one-hour workshop setting, these books are short but packed with useable information.

It's been said that there's "nothing new under the sun." Since I gratefully acknowledge the many people who taught me these concepts over more than a quarter century of homeschooling, I must also acknowledge that the concepts are not new.

These are simply the keys that opened the doors for our family. I'm happy to share them with you. I think of this book as a key ring of sorts—a place to pull many helpful thoughts and tools together so that other caring parents can access them when they need them most.

If this series were to have a dedication, I would thank the wonderful parents and educators who helped me along the way, and also honor you—the wonderful parents who are still educating and helping others.

Contents

How to Teach the Way Your Child Learns

I stand at my front door juggling an armload of groceries as I dig through my purse and coat pockets. Finally I come up with a key and shove it into the lock. It seems to fit, but no matter how I turn it, the door refuses to open.

Frustration rises the longer I stand there fumbling. I resist the urge to hurl a few choice words at the door. As if that would help...

...and then I see that *other* key on the key ring.

Obviously, it's been there all along. Why didn't I see it before?

When I try the right key, the door opens easily.

The frustration many homeschool parents experience as they try to get the doorways of understanding to open up for their child may look similar.

After digging through a pile of research on homeschooling and juggling stacks of highly recommended materials purchased online or at a local book fair, still you may feel like you're fumbling as you try to help your students get a grasp on one or more subjects.

A child's way of thinking can be like a locked door.

Could it be that we sometimes try very hard but use the wrong keys?

The Bible tells us to train up a child "in the way he should go" (Proverbs 22:6), and that's most parents' heartfelt intention, but it makes a tremendous difference which word we emphasize in that sentence. Are we supposed to train up our child in the way he *SHOULD* go? Or do we train up each child in the way *HE* should go?

In other words, must we diligently apply to children a standardized list of rules and objectives—whatever educational theory or methodology happens to be currently popular—which dictates what they *should* learn and how they *should* learn it? This interpretation seems to imply that there is one ideal key that fits all locks, and if the door does not open, something is wrong with the lock. I'm sure my personal prejudices are showing, but there's no such thing as one-size-fits-all. We don't hand out shoes or pants that way, and the results would be ridiculously unsatisfactory if we tried. "One-size-fits-all" really doesn't fit anybody very well. May I submit that a standardized, one-size-fits-all education is destined to be equally unsatisfactory?

I'd suggest that a better interpretation of Proverbs 22:6 encourages us to carefully and lovingly study each child's unique design so that we can train them in the ways they learn best for the work they were created to do.

"...we are His workmanship, created in Christ Jesus for good works, which God prepared beforehand so that we would walk in them." (Ephesians 2:10)

If we can agree that unique, individualized education is ideal, the question becomes, "How do we actually do that?" I hope this short book will help you observe and analyze the ways your child learns best and give you ideas for adapting your teaching style to the way they learn.

Five Doors into the Mind

There are five doorways into our minds: sight, hearing, touch, taste, and smell. These five senses are our means for gathering data and learning about our world. Most of us come equipped with all five, but we often depend so strongly on sight and hearing that we may neglect the other three portals of learning.

Sticking with the analogy of doorways into a home, I'm sure you'd agree that a front door makes a great first impression, but when I want to park the car and carry in groceries, the door to the garage is the most convenient route. If I'd like to access my garden or patio, I suppose I could use the front door and walk around the house and through the gate, but the back door will get me onto the patio faster.

With senses as with doors, it helps to have options.

When we're trying to get new information into our brains, it helps to know our options. The more of these learning portals we use, the richer our learning experience will be.

Why limit ourselves to just sight and hearing?

If you doubt the power of the three less-often-used senses, think of Helen Keller. Blind and deaf from infancy, she and her family were frustrated for years because she could not learn through sight and hearing like other children. Her parents were on the verge of giving up, but Helen had a brilliant mind. With the right teacher, she learned eagerly through touch, taste, and smell.

The untapped potential of all our senses working together is very powerful!

SIGHT

Sight is most people's primary means of collecting information.

When I step into a garden, for example, I notice at once the color and shape of each flower. I might see a squirrel or a hummingbird at the feeder. Looking up, I can see from the shape and color of the clouds whether we will have rain or not.

In formal learning, almost all new information is first presented visually. It's easy to include a visual aspect in learning through books, demonstrations, and videos. A captivating visual aid will reinforce your lessons even if your child is not a visual learner.

But there are sometimes challenges to visual learning.

I was an excellent student, but during the summer between 2nd and 3rd grade my family moved to a new school district. Here students were seated in alphabetical order. I sat near the back of the room because of where my name fell on the seating chart. I began to fall behind. I often raised my hand, but the teacher rarely called on me. One day I stayed after class to ask her why. She explained that there were many students who needed help. "But you're a smart girl. I know you can figure the problems out by yourself."

Trouble was, I couldn't see the assignments and examples. I couldn't read the board.

My teacher alerted my parents, who had my eyes checked, and I soon had a pair of glasses that helped a lot. But for those few months before we realized that I had a vision problem, I felt lost, invisible, and frustrated.

Good vision is a blessing. Learning through visual input is easy for a majority of people. It can be a real disadvantage to have vision that is impaired or missing, but there are other ways to collect information.

HEARING

Hearing is the second most common means of acquiring information. Most people use hearing to reinforce the visual information they receive. When I see a hummingbird at the feeder, for example, I can also hear the whir of its wings. I could hear the hummingbird even if I could not see it.

As I am writing this chapter, my back is to the window. I noticed earlier that the sky looked gray, the clouds heavy, but it was the patter of droplets on the windowpane that let me know the rain had come.

In a formal learning situation, a teacher may add an auditory component by lecturing about something the student has read in the textbook or by talking through the steps as he demonstrates how to work a mathematical equation, mix chemical ingredients, or assemble a project. The auditory part of the lesson complements and reinforces the visual portion.

For some learners and in some situations, the auditory component is primary. It may come first or be more important or have greater impact.

The act of reading aloud to a small child is an example of auditory learning as the primary means of introducing new information. The child hears the story and only later understands that the words she sees on the page are another way of telling it. Hearing is essential because she cannot fully appreciate the pleasing rhymes and rhythms, alliteration and assonance, unless she hears the way the words work together. Appealing illustrations may play an important secondary role, acting as visual aids to what the child hears, but the auditory experience of storytelling is most important.

Imagine going to a play or musical performance. Here

again there may be visual elements—costumes and sets—
that enhance the auditory experience, but in this situation
what is heard is an almost indispensable part of the
experience.

An auditory element provides great reinforcement to
any learning experience, but the auditory aspect is powerful
in its own right and should not be overlooked. If you've ever
had a song or annoying jingle "stuck in your head", you
know how effective audible learning can be in helping you
instantly recall lyrics and impressions years after you first
heard the information.

TOUCH

A baby's first experience of the world comes through touch—the texture of mama's hair, the warmth of daddy's hug, the softness of a favorite toy or blanket. Our initial experiences with touch are pleasant. Later we may learn less pleasurable lessons through touch, as I did one Christmas...

I received a shiny red bicycle when I was six and was so excited I couldn't wait for my dad to help me learn to ride it. I only intended to make an experimental run down the driveway while he got his jacket...but we lived on a hill. I wound up in my neighbor's cactus garden. That experience "sticks" in my mind as an important lesson learned through touch!

As a true child of the South, I remember learning another early lesson by sliding down a metal slide in short pants on a hot summer day. Unfortunately it took many trips down the slide to truly learn from the experience and devise a solution.

Children, especially boys, retain their dependence on touch for learning well into their teens, but too often teachers eliminate the element of touch when they present a lesson. Why? Perhaps because tactile experiences can be messy or difficult to control. We lose much, though, when we leave touch out. Touch makes a powerful impact! Touching, feeling, getting our hands dirty...tactile experiences bring learning to life.

Tactile experiences also make learning more personal. When I read or hear a lesson presented, I'm taking someone else's word for it, but when I am involved in doing something myself, my experience becomes personal— something I have done myself—and is therefore much more memorable.

Why not capitalize on the power of touch whenever we can? Teach math facts using a hopscotch number line. Snap Legos together to make a stick of ten units then break it apart to help children understand the mathematical concepts of carrying and borrowing. Students can learn an immense amount from collecting samples of rocks, shells, plants, insects, and arrowheads that they can hold in their hands. One of my children's favorite biology classes featured specimens of brains, tongues, and intestines that came from the meat department at our grocery store.

It may be tempting to eliminate the messier hands-on projects, but there is an extra measure of fascination in what I call the "Ewww!" factor that seems to delight children—and what is delightful is memorable.

TASTE

The sense of taste is another source of data input we frequently overlook, but it can add a layer of fun and richness to learning experiences. Whether the connection is direct or indirect, it's always in "good taste" to work in some fun.

When my kids' biology teacher brought sugar cookies to class and allowed the children to decorate them with the elements of a cell—"cytoplasm" jelly glaze inside a piped frosting "cell membrane" with small candies as the "nucleus", "ribosomes", and "mitochondrion"—that was a wonderful example of using taste to indirectly enhance a lesson.

Here are just a few examples of taste used as a direct data resource:

- Touching our tongues with bits of apple, lemon, and onion to find which areas are more sensitive to sweets, to sours, and to savory tastes
- Eating out at a Greek restaurant to conclude our study of Greek history and mythology
- Sampling Christmas cookies as we learned about European holiday traditions
- Tasting jerky, pemmican, and cactus jelly as we learned about native American cultures and talked about how food was preserved without refrigeration or canning
- Eating roast fowl and grease-smeared brown bread with our fingers at a medieval dinner after reading Ivanhoe

Taste is a very memorable experience that can unlock the door to other related information.

SMELL

Last but not least, smell is the most frequently overlooked sense but may be the most powerful in terms of evoking memories. Have you ever walked in a pine forest? Danced in the rain? Tilled fresh earth? Harvested sun-warmed peaches?

I have only to smell a turkey roasting, and my mouth begins to water. Instantly I am back in my grandmother's kitchen, and I can see everything else that's on the table— her china pattern, the best glasses, the relish tray. I can tell you who was there for the holiday meal and remember the things we said and did on that day. All of those related memories are attached to one simple olfactory cue.

The sense of smell can also be valuable in providing primary information, if we're paying attention. For example, doctors tell us that some diseases have a very characteristic odor. They can sometimes use the smell of the sickroom as an important clue to diagnosis. Chicken pox does not smell the same as strep any more than a rose smells like a marigold. While olfactory input may not be conclusive, it can provide good hints. We can smell rain on the wind a long time before we hear the thunder.

I grew up near the southern border of Texas. Spring, to me, smelled like tortillas because the wind shifted and blew from the south at about the same time warm weather forced the ladies across the border to take their hot cooking functions outside. I still associate the smell of tortillas baking with the coming of spring.

The ocean has a distinct smell, as does an oil field.

Try to include and call attention to olfactory elements whenever possible, because the sense of smell holds bits of information together like Super Glue!

Notes to Self

Three Learning Styles

There are three basic styles of learning: Visual, Auditory, and Physical.

You may already know your own learning style, at least on an intuitive level. It helps to know your child's learning style, too—especially if your style and your child's don't match.

For several years our family lived in Germany. When we first arrived, it was not uncommon for someone to approach me and begin speaking in German. My blank expression must have been obvious, because it usually didn't take long for the speaker to clue in that I did not understand what they were saying.

What happened next always amused me. The person trying to communicate with me would begin to speak LOUDLY and S...L...O...W...L...Y...

As if that helped!

I'm not deaf, nor am I stupid. I'm just not German.

If communication is to take place, it helps if the speaker and the hearer both use the same language!

The same is true with learning styles. If you are a visual learner and your child is an auditory or physical learner, one of you is going to have to learn to translate into a means of communicating that the other can easily understand.

Most of us show a strong preference for one of these learning styles over the others. Let's look at the traits of each learning style, then look at tools you can use to tailor your teaching methods to your students' strengths.

It's not that difficult, really, when you understand how they think.

VISUAL LEARNERS

Visual learners learn and retain best what they see. For example they tend to be prolific readers, whether reading for information or for pleasure. When I say that they are prolific, I mean that they enjoy reading and read often. I do not necessarily mean that they read quickly. Some do. Some don't. If your visual learner reads slowly, they may be taking time to learn facts or visualize images and scenes as they read. Information gained and stored in this way sticks with them because they tend to think in pictures and patterns.

Visual learners are usually very attentive. Even as babies and small children they are keen observers, able to pick up clues and nuances from their environment, from body language, and from facial expressions. Visual learners usually have an excellent grasp of direction, scale, and spatial relationships, though it may be difficult to explain those things to others because the knowledge is so intuitive to them that they're not sure how to walk anyone else through the process.

When you work with a visual learner, it will help to seat them where they can see well.

Whenever possible use visual aids to support what you are teaching:
- Pictures
- Drawings
- Graphics
- Graphs
- Diagrams
- Charts
- Flowcharts
- Illustrations
- Videos

Allow and encourage visual learners to take notes or record their observations in some way, whether they're writing down the key points of a lecture to remember later or taking photographs of what they see on a nature hike. Making sketches or even doodling can be a way of forming memory cues or expressing mental connections. Storyboarding and idea webs are ways for visual learners to capture the ideas they see vividly in their imagination. The process of outlining—seeing how a complex topic or story breaks down into parts and how those parts relate to the whole—is wonderfully helpful for visual learners.

When the student has to memorize material or review for a test, it is helpful for them to review their own written notes. Outlining and flash cards are other great review tools for visual learners.

Visual learners have a distinct advantage when it comes to taking tests because they tend to perform very well on written tests—the type of tests most frequently given in large group settings.

AUDITORY LEARNERS

Auditory learners would rather attend a lecture than read a book. These students love to be read to. (Actually, almost all children love to be read to. Oral reading is one of the greatest things you can do for your children, providing unbelievable benefits to them later in life.) When they're old enough to read for themselves, auditory learners may still enjoy reading aloud, even if only to themselves. They may also subvocalize, whispering or "muttering" the words softly to themselves when they think they're reading silently. Written information may not "stick" until they hear it.

Auditory learners may also enjoy rhythm and repetition. Do you have a little one who hums constantly or beats rhythms? Do they play with words and the sounds they make? These are fun activities for auditory learners that can be harnessed for learning. Auditory learners tend to pick up on subtext—the underlying meanings of what we say—through cues in tone of voice, pitch, speed or other nuances. Background noise may be distracting to auditory learners OR it may aid in focus.

"Vince" is an example of an auditory learner who became a gifted attorney and college lecturer. As a student, Vince likely studied with music playing as "white noise" to block out random distractions. As an adult, he noticed that he formed associations between the songs that were playing and the subjects he was studying at the time. As a lecturer, he began to memorize his speeches while listening to albums, creating deliberate memory cues. At the end of a semester, his class could ask him any question, and after humming a few bars he was able to give them the answer, quoting verbatim from a lecture he delivered months before.

Because auditory learners retain best what they learn by listening, try to include an auditory element to reach them.
- Lectures
- Ranger talks
- Historic re-enactments with interactive docents
- Read-aloud sessions
- Audio books
- Songs to teach the alphabet, numbers, grammar, geography (think: Schoolhouse Rock)
- Catchy rhythms, rhymes, or alliteration (lists that start with the same sounds)
- Podcasts
- Listen to period music as you study history
- Special trips to the symphony or other musical performance

Let audio learners memorize to music or beat out a rhythm when there are facts to be remembered. (These guys never forget a jingle!) If you look, you can find commercially produced songs to teach states and capitols, nations and continents, Bible verses, math facts and phonics rules. Or you might try writing your own.

When my children were small, we had fun inventing our own silly songs. For example, we learned the geographic features of the Arabian Peninsula, in order, to the tune of the French "Can-Can" song. To this day, we can't hear that tune without smiling, and someone will eventually begin to sing: "Turkey, Cypress, Syria...Lebanon and Israel...Jordan, Iraq, and Iran...Kuwait, Saudi Arabia...United Arab Emirates...Qatar, Oman, and Yemen...Black Sea, Caspian, Persian Gulf...Arabian, Red Sea, Med!" We remember every country and sea almost TWENTY YEARS LATER!

As an example of rhythm, we created "rap" songs to learn the major Egyptian rulers:

"Hapshetsut was the queen...
First woman to rule the scene.
Hapshetsut! Hapshetsut!
She built no pyramid.
Temple-building's what she did.
Hapshetsut! Hapshetsut!"

The ditty can be simple—even silly—and still be effective.

Auditory learners also benefit from a Socratic teaching method where they can shadow a mentor, ask questions, and talk through the answers.

Whenever possible, let your audio learner record lecture notes with a recording device rather than requiring them to always take written notes. This will allow them to give the lecture their full attention, and notes that can be played back and listened to again and again will be of far more use to them.

When studying for exams, oral exercises such as peer reviews, focus groups, or question and answer sessions are ideal for auditory learners.

Auditory learners perform best on oral quizzes. I always cringe when people ask if my Discover Texas curriculum has tests they can print out. It does, and written tests work great for visual learners, but if you want to get the truest idea of how well your auditory learner has understood the material, let them tell you about what they've learned. Lead them in discussion questions. Who says a test has to be written to be valid? Where did we get the idea that any other type of test is merely an "accommodation" for a student with "learning differences"? We *all* learn differently! Doesn't a candidate for a doctoral degree defend his dissertation orally? Certainly it requires a good deal of knowledge and communication skills to think on one's feet and give a clear and thorough answer. This is where auditory learners shine.

PHYSICAL LEARNERS

Physical learners learn best while doing and retain best when they are active in the learning process. If you have a student who seems to constantly wiggle—fidgeting in their seat, swinging their legs, tapping a pencil, jouncing one foot, or contorting their body as they concentrate on a task—you are very likely looking at a physical learner.

Almost all very young children are physical learners to some degree, and boys tend to learn actively longer than girls do. In fact, I've taught several high school boys who were still physical learners at sixteen or seventeen. Physical learners typically find it difficult to sit still for long periods. This may explain why boys are more likely than girls to get in trouble for causing a disturbance in traditional classrooms and why many young men look back on their school days as a benign form of torture.

My husband spent several years teaching computer design and networking at a technical college. Many of his students did not view themselves as "college material", usually because they had not performed very well in high school classes. They lacked confidence in their ability to complete even a two-year degree, but once they got their hands on machines and wiring, they were in their intuitive element! Most were surprised to learn that a technical career could earn a very gratifying salary. A mature physical learner is a master craftsman!

Physical learners are often differentiated as **tactile (small muscle) learners** or **kinetic (large muscle) learners**. Tactile learners like to feel things—textures, shapes, and consistencies—and usually have a high degree of dexterity and fine motor skills. Kinetic learners like to expend energy and actively participate as they learn. These students often excel in athletic pursuits.

Both tactile and kinetic learners are highly sensory. They are adventurers and risk takers. Physical learners enjoy practical activities—preferably activities that serve a purpose. Hands-on experiences aid tremendously in their retention.

When you teach physical learners, it is important to let them move! Incorporate physical activity into your lessons.

- Give a live demonstration then let them try
- Conduct lab experiments, and let them get their hands in it
- Take field trips
- Use manipulatives
- Make models
- Do arts and crafts
- Cook
- Assign projects
- Give them practical activities
- Consider an apprenticeship in their field of interest

Because physical learners learn best by doing, they enjoy creating things that others can appreciate. You can tap into this and help them learn by giving them opportunities to teach others through a model or diorama they've made, by performing a skit or play, or perhaps by putting together a video presentation.

Tests can be daunting for physical learners. They're best at showing you what they've learned on a practicum. Help them see that this is NOT merely an accommodation for some perceived weakness. Physicians and engineers are often required to take a practicum to prove their competency. Unfortunately this is not the type of test that's most convenient for large groups, so at some point physical learners will have to develop a tolerance for written tests, but while they are learning in a smaller, less formal setting you can help them build confidence by testing their knowledge in ways that come naturally to them.

Just as it's possible to learn another language, your child will eventually become more skilled at understanding different teaching styles and performing well on a variety of tests. But especially when introducing new material, it will be much easier for a student to concentrate on the lesson when it's presented in his "native language" style. One of the advantages of a home school setting is that we can accommodate learning differences in the ways we teach and test until our students build confidence in their abilities. With confidence in their abilities, the transition to standard written testing forms should be much smoother.

Notes to Self

Knowing Your Own Learning Style

As you read through these descriptions with your child's learning style in mind, you may have identified your own, as well. The parent's learning style greatly affects their teaching style, because we naturally teach in the way that seems easiest for us to learn.

That may or may not be the easiest way for your child to learn, though. Or it may be the way one of your children learns, but another may learn entirely differently.

Your learning style is part of you. It's part of the uniqueness that makes you who you are. You can't change your preferred learning style, and your child can't change his or hers...but you *can* change your teaching style. As the adult, you have more understanding of what's going on and a more mature ability to adapt.

We might think of education as a relay where one runner passes the baton of knowledge to the teammate who will run the next lap. The baton pass may be the most critical step of the race. Time can be made up over the course, but each runner must pass the baton in such a way that their teammate can grasp it firmly.

Another way to picture the education process is as a game of catch. The pitcher throws the ball in such a way that the receiver can catch it. As a student, did you ever have the unfortunate experience of an instructor who seemed to be playing maul ball instead? Perhaps the information was hurled too high or too low, too fast, or you may have been tricked by a curve ball. There is a huge difference between maul ball and a friendly game of catch—especially for the catcher! In a game of catch, you are teammates. In maul ball, you are opponents. In maul ball, you score by hitting your opponent, and if your opponent should happen to catch the ball, they will only hurl it back. In a game of catch, you score by seeing how long you can successfully continue a win-win situation.

It's important to know what kind of "receiver" our child is so we can pitch knowledge in a way that allows them to catch it. The better we are at playing this game, the more successful we'll be at creating a win-win situation.

Notes to Self

A Few Thoughts on Testing

Our word "test" comes from a Middle English word for the clay vessels in which metals were assayed (examined, assessed, evaluated, analyzed, and/or appraised) to determine their content and quality. The important part of the testing was the metal and its content, not the size or shape of the clay vessel. No one cared about the potsherds.

So why do we care so much about the form of tests used in education?

When we give a child a test over material we hope they've learned in school, the important thing is the child and the learning, *not* the test. I feel like I have to say this because so much emphasis is placed on school tests these days. A child may be labeled "a failure" if they don't satisfy a certain percentage of expected answers in exactly the way deemed acceptable. Teachers' careers teeter in jeopardy if a room full of wonderfully unique youngsters don't answer exactly the same questions in exactly the same way. School funding depends on these answers. Schools can be shut down if the required percentage of students doesn't parrot those expected and acceptable answers. In some states, testing determines whether homeschool parents may or may not retain their right as parents to continue to oversee the education of their own children. Governments and bureaucrats have imbued these tests with the powers of gods to determine the value and destinies of human beings, though the tests are written by humans and changed frequently, almost on a whim.

Tests make fickle gods.

We must remember that the end goal of any test is to establish that the student has acquired knowledge, understands the concepts, and can use their new skills proficiently when a similar situation calls for their application. If the results of the test show that they can, then we move on to the next concept. If the results of the test indicate that they cannot, then we try again. We go back and see where they are in the learning process.

- Do they remember the information?
- Did they understand the concept?
- Are they able to apply the skill in a different situation?
- Can they identify similar situations where the application of this skill is appropriate?

Too often the test becomes the end of learning. If the student does not understand, it may feel as if that big red "F" at the top of the page says, "Ah-ha! I've caught you! You're stupid! You're lazy! You didn't really try! Now the rest of us are going on, and you had better catch up." What a terrible, presumptive thing to do to a child. If they have not mastered the prerequisite concepts, how can we expect them to grasp what comes next?

Remember that we are playing catch, not maul ball. We are teammates in education trying to create a win-win situation. If our purpose in teaching is to help our child learn, then we must teach in such a way that they *can* learn. The purpose of the test it to make sure they're still with us before we proceed to the next level.

I know, I know. Most schools give written tests. But why? Because they have a large number of students to test all at once. Because they may be sending the tests off to be graded, perhaps by a machine. Because they need to keep a record. All of this makes sense for traditional schools.

One of the many advantages of homeschooling is that you have the luxury of adapting the test to the student so as to gain the clearest picture of their progress. With each child working on their own grade level, tests are administered on a very small scale. Mom usually does the grading and keeps her own records. Why can't an auditory learner be given an oral exam? Why can't a physical learner take a practicum?

What about records that may be required by the state for oversight? You could let your auditory learner read the test questions and record their answers on the computer, storing the information as MP3 files. You might use your smart phone to record or make a video recording as they give a report. You can take photos or video of your physical learner's demonstrations or save their hand-made projects as evidence of progress. Chat with your overseeing official in advance to see what other options are available as documentation.

Co-op classes or dual credit classes might present occasions where a homeschooled student would need to take a standard written test, but these typically do not come into play early in a child's experience. For an auditory or physical learner, learning to take a written test is an academic skill just like any other—something they can learn to master at an appropriate age with sufficient practice. As the parent, you may have some say in deciding if they're ready for a situation that will require written testing. Certainly you can help them practice at home in a non-threatening environment. How about reviewing for the test first in their natural learning style? This will allow them to build confidence that they do understand the material. Is it possible to take a practice test at home? Some teachers make old test files available. Others might do so upon request.

One homeschool co-op teacher gave students a copy of the chapter test at the *beginning* of each unit, only she re-titled it "Reading Guide." Students knew in advance what information the teacher considered important, and they learned to read for content—an important skill for mature readers. Answers were discussed in class, which provided auditory feedback. Students had their reading guides to review at the end of the unit. On test day each student received a blank form with the same questions. They already knew the answers. They'd now seen or reviewed them three times. The "test" was more of a "game" to see how many answers they could remember without looking. This seemed to help many students relax and do their best.

What about end-of-year achievement testing? This is a situation where a large number of students will be tested all at once, the tests will be graded by a machine, and the records need to be kept on file. It is the quintessential written test in all its bubble charted infamy, but you can still assure your child that it is just an assessment of what they've learned and how well they can apply their skills in new situations. It is a snapshot of one day in their progress. Hopefully this will take some of the pressure off so that students can do their best, and of course you can help them by making sure they get a good night's sleep, have a calm morning, and come prepared with a good hearty breakfast under their ribs.

What about the ACT and SAT? College entrance exams are a long way down the road. If you start working on test-taking skills early, especially with your auditory and physical learners, chances are they will be able to tolerate the transition to college-level test formats fairly well. A wide variety of test prep helps, and pretests are offered for both the SAT and ACT. It might also be a good idea to allow your student to take the PreSAT so they'll know what to expect. Currently, students are able to take both of these assessment tests as many times as they like if they'd like to improve their grades.

Notes to Self

How Temperament Affects Learning

There are many ways of understanding the wide diversity of personalities and temperaments and how they affect the way individuals learn. To begin we must recognize that temperament is not exactly the same thing as personality. It's helpful to think of temperament as the root motivations and social preferences from which our unique personalities grow.

The ancient Greeks summarized four basic temperaments. Some modern psychologists use a similar system, devising a matrix that gauges extrovert and introvert tendencies as well as describing whether individuals tend to be more goal-oriented or relationship-driven. On the most basic level, this matrix sorts social preferences and motivations.

Before we go further, I want to emphasize that these are definitely generalizations on a sliding-scale continuum.

Social preferences refer not so much to friendliness and self-confidence as to the source of our inspiration and energy. Extroverts are energized and inspired in a stimulating, active, social environment—one external to themselves. Introverts find energy and inspiration in a quiet, relaxed, reflective environment, often alone or with a very small, intimate circle of trusted friends.

Motivation refers to the primary concern in problem-solving and decision-making. Again I want to emphasize that both goal-oriented and relationship-oriented people may be very friendly and confident, but goal-oriented temperaments tend to keep one eye always on the ultimate goal or purpose of their actions while relationship-oriented temperaments tend to prioritize the way actions affect community.

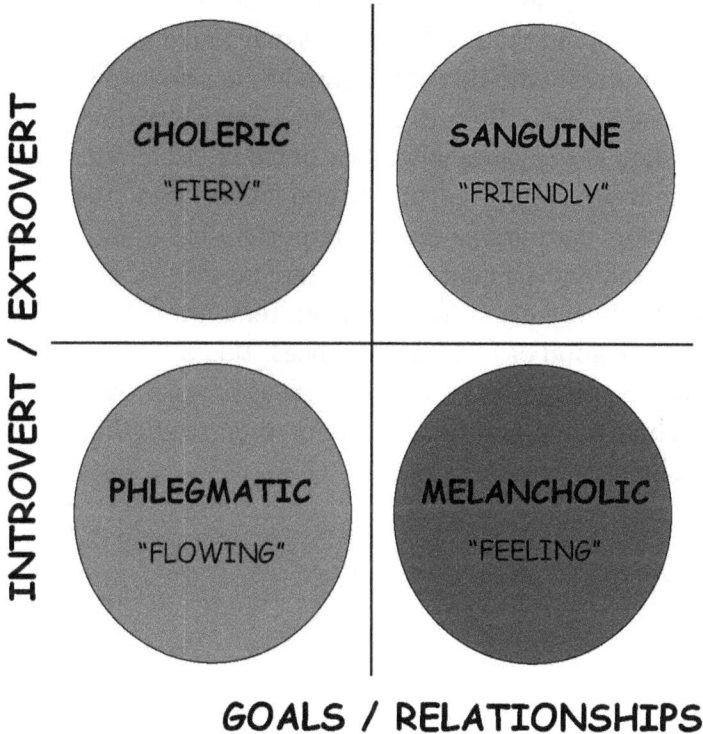

INTROVERT / EXTROVERT

CHOLERIC
"FIERY"

SANGUINE
"FRIENDLY"

PHLEGMATIC
"FLOWING"

MELANCHOLIC
"FEELING"

GOALS / RELATIONSHIPS

There is no "right" or "wrong" to temperaments. Each has strengths and weaknesses. Each of us has a unique blend in varying degrees, though one temperament will usually be predominant. With the understanding that these tendencies are neither positive nor negative, neither good nor bad, we can proceed to recognize patterns that may help us tailor our teaching to our children.

Your child's temperament is part of what makes him or her unique. As temperament pertains to learning, understanding your child's comfort zone, strengths and challenges may help you tailor their learning environment and give them opportunities to shine.

As with learning styles, it's also important to consider that temperament affects both the teacher and the student, the parent and the child. Teachers may find it easier to work with students who think and learn in the same ways they do. (It's always easier to communicate when we're not trying to translate at the same time.) Our personal preferences may cause us to admire some traits and find other quirks and behaviors undesirable, but it's important to remember that temperament is a neutral characteristic—neither good nor bad. It's how we choose to USE our temperament that results in good or bad consequences. This will become clearer as we go along, but our goal as parents and teachers is to help our students capitalize on their strengths and modify their weaknesses.

CHOLERICS

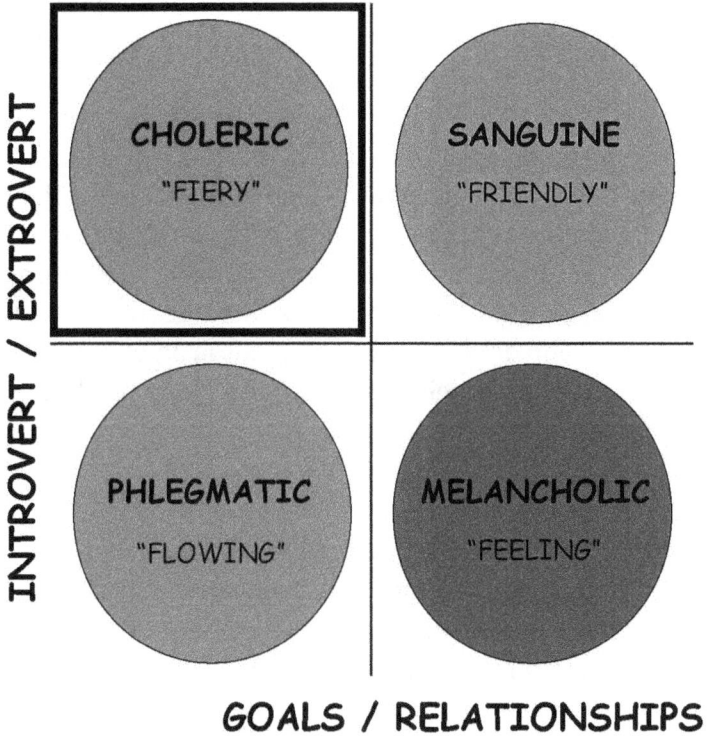

CHOLERIC

"FIERY"

SANGUINE

"FRIENDLY"

PHLEGMATIC

"FLOWING"

MELANCHOLIC

"FEELING"

INTROVERT / EXTROVERT

GOALS / RELATIONSHIPS

People with a choleric temperament are goal-oriented extroverts.

Characteristics of the "Fiery" Cholerics:
- Energized and inspired in a stimulating, active, social environment
- Strong leaders
- Need to know what the goal is and who's in charge
- Crave structure
- Love a challenge
- Efficient process people
- Strong finishers

On the downside, they may become easily bored if they sense no clear purpose or feel frustrated if progress bogs down. Since they are strong leaders, they may come off as "bossy" or "rebellious", but actually they don't always feel the need to lead as long as someone they respect is in charge. Like good soldiers, these students actually follow directions faithfully once you've won their respect. If they're part of a team effort, they'll be the ones working hardest, leading by example, and shouting encouragements. Properly challenged, you can usually count on them to initiate with enthusiasm and drive toward their goals in an efficient manner (sometimes being a bit of a "bulldozer" perhaps). They don't understand the concept of quitting.

To teach a choleric student effectively, you must:
- Win their respect
- Present a clearly defined purpose with checkpoints and deadlines, if possible, so they'll know what's expected
- Give them responsibility/put them in charge of something
- "Stretch" and inspire them
- Allow opportunities to compete with others or with their own past performance
- Praise their accomplishments

Nurtured in a godly environment, this temperament type usually develops into a leader or guardian. Most people can easily see boys of this temperament becoming military officers or CEOs, but a godly woman with strong leadership qualities can become an awesome model of strength and beauty, as well.

SANGUINES

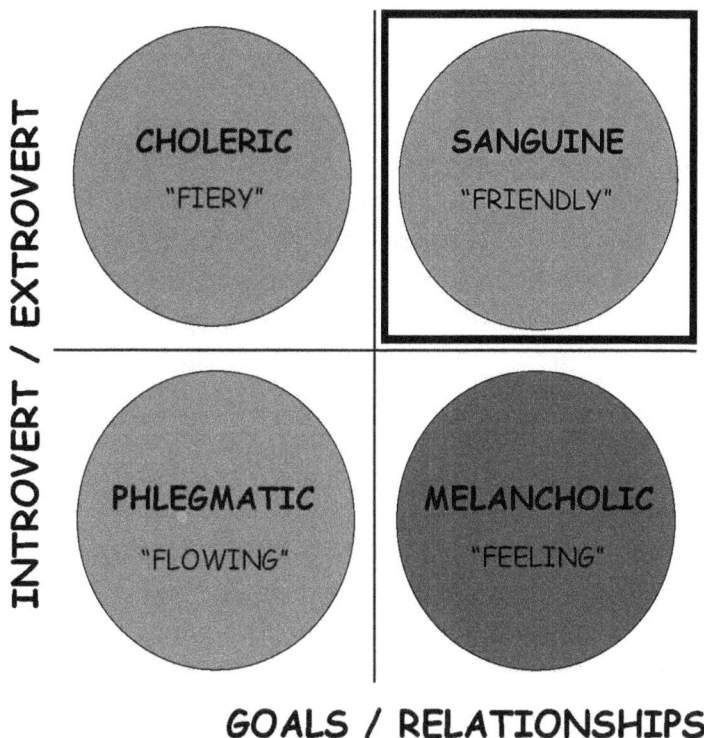

People with the sanguine temperament are relationship-oriented extroverts.

Characteristics of the "Friendly" Sanguines:
- Energized and inspired in a stimulating, active, social environment
- Energetic, playful, inter-relational
- Need to know when the fun starts
- Crave variety, surprise, and adventure
- Great team players, they inspire others
- Need to interact and process information by talking
- Generate tons of ideas

These kids can be "the life of the party," but the drawback may be that "if it's not fun, they're done." They have tons of energy. It's a challenge to keep them busy, but once they're bored, they lose interest quickly. Optimists by nature, they find joy in small things and share generously. (If you're trying to keep a group focused on the task at hand, this is not always a good thing.) They tend to process externally and orally, so they may ask TONS of questions, chatter with their neighbor, or leave you in the dust when their active minds shoot off in some tangent direction that may not seem related, but don't write them off as "light-weights" by any means. They can generate more ideas than they can ever complete in three lifetimes. They make friends easily, though they may have to develop wisdom and discernment in this area through painful experiences. They have huge hearts and are naturally gifted at building teams and inspiring action. They can "get the ball rolling" for sure...but they may need others on the team to help them finish. (Finishing complex tasks can be a REAL challenge to people of this temperament.)

To teach sanguine students effectively, you must:
- Keep things interesting, surprising and fun
- Give them outlets to work and play with others frequently
- Let them concentrate in short, focused bursts interspersed with activity
- Let them talk and ask questions
- Let them generate ideas, but help them analyze for priority and practicality
- Break complex tasks into smaller goals and celebrate the completion of each
  Nurtured in a godly environment, people with this type

of temperament are usually known for their optimism, generosity and kind hearts. Their social skills will take them far.

MELANCHOLICS

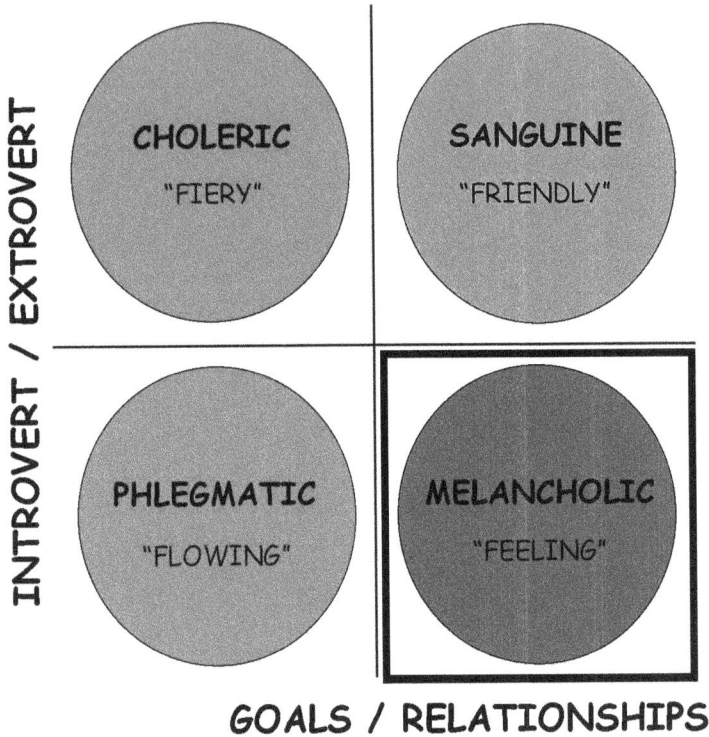

INTROVERT / EXTROVERT

| CHOLERIC "FIERY" | SANGUINE "FRIENDLY" |
| PHLEGMATIC "FLOWING" | MELANCHOLIC "FEELING" |

GOALS / RELATIONSHIPS

People with the deep-feeling melancholic temperament are relationship-oriented introverts.

Characteristics of the "Feeling" Melancholics:
- Energized and inspired in a quiet, relaxed, reflective environment
- Great "big picture" vision
- Need to know why and what if
- Crave imaginative expression
- Love an opportunity to create
- Need time to process information and generate connections

- Intuitive encouragers

Artistic melancholics tend to spend a lot of time inside their own heads…and the alternate universe in there is astounding! (I tell you this from personal experience. *wink*) They DO like people, and it's not entirely accurate to think of them as shy since they may have a healthy self-image and quite a lot to say, but they may find large group interaction stressful. That's not to say they don't like to socialize, but they usually prefer routine and solitude and need generous doses of quiet to balance "social noise." They tend to be perfectionists, so encouragement and approval is essential. Trust them to surprise you by exceeding expectations, but realize that quality takes time.

To teach melancholic students effectively, you must:
- Give them time to mull things over and consider how disciplines interrelate
- Invite them to contribute to group efforts, but do not force group projects
- Let them experiment with different forms of artistic expression
- Let them invent and/or create as a way to reflect what they've learned
- Correct and advise, but do it gently! These perfectionists wither under harsh criticism or false praise

Nurtured in a godly environment, people with this temperament type are natural nurturers who use their rich imaginations to create beauty and enrich the lives of others. As children, they may be like butterflies—flourishing in a rather small cocoon, but don't worry. They'll come out when they're ready, and they'll fly beautifully.

PHLEGMATICS

CHOLERIC
"FIERY"

SANGUINE
"FRIENDLY"

PHLEGMATIC
"FLOWING"

MELANCHOLIC
"FEELING"

INTROVERT / EXTROVERT

GOALS / RELATIONSHIPS

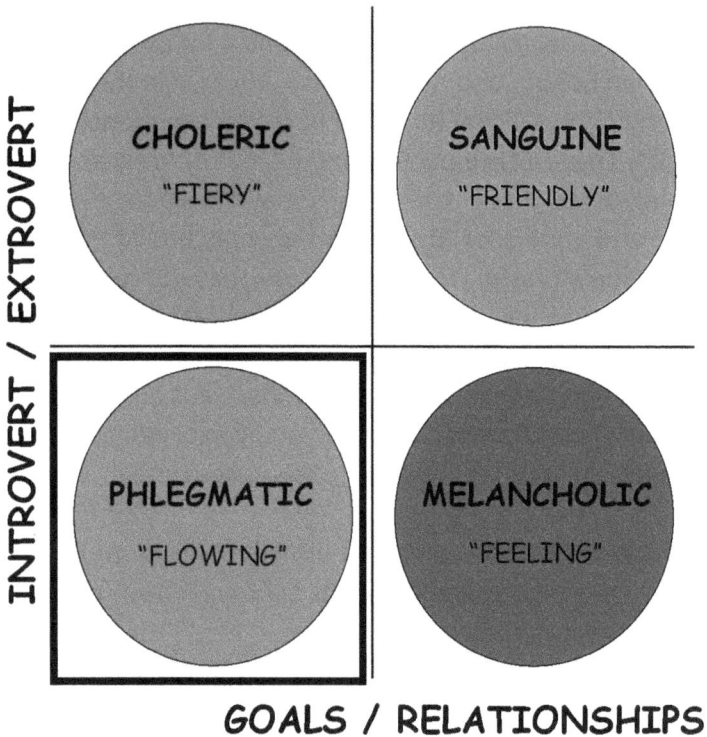

Quiet and diligent, people with the smooth-flowing phlegmatic temperament are goal-oriented introverts.

Characteristics of the "Flowing" Phlegmatics:
- Energized and inspired in a quiet, relaxed, reflective environment
- Practical, stable, dependable—they are the glue that works invisibly to hold things together
- Need to know what the purpose is, how you'd like it done, and when it's due
- Crave structure
- Want a deadline and will finish early to allow time to

check their work
- Efficient process people
- Strong finishers

You may have noticed that this type of person shares many traits with the fiery, extroverted leader types, but they are MUCH more quiet. They will go out of their way to avoid conflict and do not enjoy leading, though their gifts of organization, attention to detail, and knack for scheduling actually equips them well for leadership. (George Washington is a famous example of a strong phlegmatic leader—wise and much-loved.) Unflappable, this type of person is sometimes mischaracterized as a "plodder". They tend to progress slowly and deliberately. Don't rush them, or you may witness a melt-down as they try to meet your demands while satisfying their own desire for flawless perfection! Decision-making is sometimes a challenge because they like to make sure they have all the facts and reduce all possible risks before committing, but once they set a course, they will work diligently and steadily and finish dependably.

To teach phlegmatic students effectively, you must:
- Let them know the goals and objectives of an assignment
- Help them see how skills will be practical and useful to them later in life
- Let them know when assignments are due and allow time for them to check their work
- Be prepared for them to break large tasks into manageable segments. They tend to do this naturally.
- Encourage them that their ideas and skills are valuable so they will learn to speak up in groups.

Nurtured in a godly environment, people with this temperament type are gentle, caring, and rock-steady. They live to serve in practical ways and take immense satisfaction in a job well done. Naturally modest, you don't have to worry too much that they will become arrogant, so be sure to let them know when you're pleased.

Notes to Self

Seven Natural Intelligences

When we think of someone who's creative, our minds might first go to a painter or musician, an actor or a novelist. But creativity takes myriad forms...

- What about the homemaker who creates amazing meals on a budget? Or comes up with storage solutions that keep the household organized?
- What about the gardener who invented raised beds to make gardening more enjoyable?
- How about architects, builders, and engineers who use their creativity to give us homes, buildings, bridges, roads, etc. that are both functional and beautiful?
- How about the mathematicians and computer programmers who devise "dummy-proof" charts and programs that anyone can use to make budgeting and routine processes easier?
- Come to think of it, what about teachers who devise innovative ways of making learning meaningful, memorable and fun?

Steve Jobs, the creative genius behind Apple computers, once said, "Creativity is just connecting things. When you ask creative people how they did something, they feel a little guilty because they didn't really do it, they just saw something."

Formal schooling tends to focus primarily on skills that are language-related (reading, writing, literature) or mathematics-related (arithmetic and science). A student who excels in these two areas is rewarded with high marks. In addition, students who excel in certain sports may win recognition and admiration. But these are just three of at least seven distinct natural intelligences—seven types of "genius." If your child has one or more of the less-recognized talents, they may not recognize that they actually have "hidden superpowers"!

Part of raising up a child "in the way HE should go" is studying to see the areas in which his or her creative process begins to shine. Let's look at some of the areas where your child might be gifted and talented.

VERBAL

People with verbal intelligence have a gift for words, whether they're avid readers, writers, or speakers. They're storytellers. They enjoy playing with words—puns, puzzles, humor, analogies, rhymes...you name it. Their language is expressive and persuasive. They have a way of putting things that makes you feel their message, a way of explaining things that makes concepts clearer.

If you have a wonderful wordsmith at your house, how can you encourage them to grow in their gift?

Equip them with books of all kinds—fiction, non-fiction, poetry, biographies—and let them bask in worthy inspiration.

Play word games. My mom did this with us from the time we were very young. While we were driving in the car, washing dishes, or weeding the garden, she'd say a word, and we'd try to think of words that rhymed. Sometimes we'd adapt the game and think of synonyms or antonyms. Other times we'd choose a topic—names, places, animals, foods, or colors—and take turns thinking of related words in alphabetical order. It was a great way to build vocabulary!

Word puzzles of all kinds can hone skills and build confidence. If your verbal genius conquers these too quickly, let him design some of his own.

Let them start a collection of idioms, expressions, or wise and witty sayings.

"Calligraphy" literally means "beautiful writing". Let wordsmiths try their hand at creating word art or unique fonts. There may be a calligraphy guild in your area, but if not, you can find other "beautiful writers" on social media forums such as Pinterest.

Provide your verbally gifted child with writing tools—

plenty of paper, pencils, pens. There's a whole world of luxurious craft papers, handmade journals, free fonts and amazing calligraphic tools out there that will make their fingers itch and their imaginations tingle! Let them learn how to use writing tools on the computer, too—Word, Publisher, and PowerPoint are good starters.

Encourage them to keep a diary, find a pen pal, or write to an imaginary friend. When I was a little girl, I wrote letters, wrapped them in waterproof coverings, and dropped them down into the trunk of a hollow tree. I loved imagining who might find my written time capsules later.

Let them tell stories.

Help your storyteller learn to look for story ideas. My third-grade teacher encouraged my love of writing by presenting me with a workbook full of fanciful illustrations. My job was to write stories about what might be happening in the pictures. I read recently about another teacher who helped her second graders find the seeds of story ideas by giving them tiny notebooks hung on bright ribbon necklaces so they could record "Tiny Topics" from their day to use as writing prompts later. Once your budding writer learns that the seeds for stories are literally everywhere, be prepared for creativity to bloom.

Wordsmiths aren't always writers. Sometimes they're speakers. It can be a challenge to find outlets to develop speaking skills, but perhaps your church or community has a civic theater. Let them volunteer for read-alouds at your local library or book store. Check out the nearest chapter of Toastmasters. Get active in a mock trial or debate program. Let them experiment with making movies or recordings. And always, always discuss and dialogue within your family!

VISUAL/SPATIAL

Do you have a budding artist, architect, or engineer in your house? A little one who builds forts or fairy houses in the back yard, plays happily with LEGOs for hours on end, or draws with incredible detail but cries in frustration because it "still doesn't look right" (when it looks perfectly fine to you)? If so, you may have a child with high visual/spatial intelligence.

People with visual and/or spatial superpowers have great imaginations. They can "see" the finished product in their minds before they ever pick up a pencil. Remember those test questions that ask, "If you fold this shape, which box will it look like?" They can figure those out fairly quickly, because they're adept at visualizing and manipulating images. They have heightened spatial awareness which sometimes translates into a "bat-like" sense of navigation. (They rarely get lost but may actually feel dizzy for a while if you rearrange the furniture.) These kids have an unusual awareness of lines, shapes, and forms that naturally expresses itself through designing, drawing, or doodling.

The gift comes naturally, but they need practice and experience to make their plans a reality. Here are some activities that can help:

Let them play with puzzles and mazes.

Expose them to inspiring examples of art—not just museum-quality paintings and sculptures, but everyday art forms such as quilting, sewing, cake baking, or toy making.

Give them lots of art tools to experiment with–crayons, pens, pencils, paints, drawing paper, construction paper, watercolor, pastel chalks, clay, wood, textiles, and LEGOs. If possible, you might set aside a special shelf, drawer, closet, or even an under-bed storage container for craft supplies.

You never know what art form may be "just right" for them.

Let them experiment with photography and video cameras, since art is not always static.

Play imaginative games. "If you can dream it, you can do it"...but first you have to dream it. Walt Disney called this "Imagineering", but like any skill it takes time and practice. This time is not wasted. Daydreaming and playing ARE the work of children.

PHYSICAL

People with natural body awareness and coordination may not even be aware of their gift. It's easy to take for granted and easy to overlook since we don't typically "test" physical prowess like we do other school subjects, but those of us who lack physical and athletic skills can assure you they don't come naturally to everyone! Physical "geniuses" have natural grace, flexibility, balance, strength and/or speed. They may use their bodies to express ideas and emotions and may communicate best with touch and gesture.

Physical superpowers sometimes show up very early. My nephew's first word was, "Ball!" and his enthusiasm for sports has never waned.

Whether your physical genius is an athlete, actor, gymnast, or ballerina, help them build on their natural gifts by giving them tactile experiences from an early age. The talent may come naturally, but the strength and skills are honed over time.

As they grow, give kids with physical intelligence as many opportunities as you can to learn in motion. Unit studies, for example, will capitalize on their preference for hands-on learning.

Give them opportunities to build and create on large and small scales.

Let them engage in dramatic role play, interpreting history, literature, and music through motion.

Above all let them engage in sports, games, and physical activity. For a child who is "all about physical activity," sitting still and quiet in a chair for eight hours can feel like torture.

"The mind can only absorb what the seat can endure."

MUSICAL

A person with "musical genius" will often show awareness of melody and rhythm from a very early age—sometimes even *in utero*. Before she was born, our daughter surprised me at a concert by kicking in perfect time to the music. These tiny musicians begin by responding to music, swaying or tapping rhythms with hands and feet. Look for this to continue through childhood. Those little guys who are always singing, humming, whistling, or using their pencils to drum on the desk? Yeah. Them. But don't let it irritate you. These kids tend to have an innate understanding of musical structure. They can definitely carry a tune—even without a bucket. Music and rhythm are their means of communication and their gift to the world.

So how do you develop a budding Beethoven or Bo Diddley?

Expose them to a broad spectrum of musical inspiration. As with other forms of art, there's a wide variety of styles...and many more haven't been invented yet!

Sing-alongs can be great fun whether your family sings along to movie scores, sings silly car songs, or joins your community's annual presentation of The Messiah or a church cantata.

Songs can also be a great way to memorize school material—the alphabet, states and capitols, world geography, math facts, or Bible verses.

When the time is right, expose your little Mozart to a variety of musical instruments. Let them experiment and, if possible, provide music lessons on an instrument they show interest in playing.

Above all (and this is true of EVERY gift) encourage their early efforts! Do NOT critique each performance. It takes time to get "what's inside" to "come outside" in the same form and to become comfortable exercising your gifts in front of others. Just relax and enjoy, and the skill will develop.

MATHEMATICAL

Referring to this group as "mathematical geniuses" is a bit of a misnomer. Sure, they're good at math, but more than that, they're good at thinking logically. They "get" systems—number systems, organizational systems, even biological systems make intuitive sense to them. They easily see ways to organize and categorize things into efficient patterns. Cause and effect relationships are readily apparent to them—so much so that they can spot clues and use deductive reasoning to infer what came before and what will follow. Taking those skills another step, they may become skilled at pre-direction—deliberately making choices that will insure the best probability of good outcomes.

It goes without saying that they're killer-good at puzzles.

So how do you mentor a mathematician?

Give them problems to solve!

Manipulatives make math meaningful. Use LEGOs, coins, candies, dice, cards, and other household items to illustrate the logic of new ideas in math.

And don't stop with arithmetic. Think "science." Biology is the study of physical systems. Astronomy is the study of celestial systems. Meteorology is the study of weather systems. Mathematical equations and cause-and-effect relationships are a huge component of both chemistry and genetics. Even physics is basically "God playing with math." Give your logic-minded student access to science materials and magazines, and make room for the growing collections of experiments and specimens that are sure to follow. (They can probably handle the organization of said collections themselves.)

Is there a science museum nearby? That would make an excellent field trip, as would family outings such as nature hikes and stargazing.

To take advantage of their pre-directive skills, why not let them read the biographies of great mathematicians, scientists, and physicians? Insight into how others have looked at the world and seen new possibilities is great inspiration!

As an interesting side note, there is often a correlation between mathematicians, scientists, and musicians. Music is a highly developed system with a logical basis in mathematics, so if your child has mathematical superpowers, watch to see if there's a musical aspect as well.

MOTIVATIONAL

Many educators break this category down into **Introspective** and **Interpersonal** skills, but I chose to lump these superpowers together because whether your student is "Self" smart (Introspective) or "Social" smart (Interpersonal), the root skill is the same. Introverted or extroverted, these people understand what makes human beings "tick" and use that knowledge to motivate themselves and others. They are world-changers.

A person who is **Introspective/"Self" smart** is in tune with their own emotions, motivations, strengths and weaknesses. They usually demonstrate an exceptional ability to focus. As they mature, they become sensitive, by extension, to the emotions, strengths, and struggles of others.

Inclined to be a bit solitary when they're young, people with this superpower often become empathetic friends and wise counselors.

Equip them with secret places, time alone, self-paced projects, and opportunities to make choices.

A person who is **Interpersonal/"Social" smart** understands and relates well to others and communicates effectively. They seldom have difficulty remembering names and faces and seem comfortable talking to people from all walks of life.

My niece demonstrated this superpower one Christmas Eve when a frantic husband entered the dress shop where she worked needing to find a last-minute extra gift for his wife. My niece, who seems to know everyone in town, was well-acquainted with his wife and able to help him find not only the right size but the colors and styles of clothing she preferred. The man was thrilled to purchase an entire ensemble, complete with purse, scarf, and earrings!

There's a good chance people with this superpower will find their calling in roles that require a personal touch, a helpful spirit, or team-building skills.

Equip them with community activities, clubs (whether they join them, lead them, or start them), apprenticeship under a mentor, and opportunities to contribute and lead.

Like the Physical "geniuses", Motivational "geniuses" may not recognize their own gift, and it is often easily overlooked by others. It may be up to you to study and recognize their special abilities to motivate themselves and others and channel them into opportunities to make a real difference in the areas they care about.

ENVIRONMENTAL

The best way I know how to explain this gift is by giving you two stories as examples.

One day as we were leaving the house, my 7-year-old son advised me to bring an umbrella. Puzzled, I said, "It's not going to rain. There's not a cloud in the sky," to which he answered, "There were clouds yesterday—those little wooly ones that look like fish scales. When you see those, it usually rains the next day." And it did. I was glad I went back for the umbrella!

While driving I pointed out something I thought would be of interest to the same kiddo. "Oh, look! An armadillo!" He replied (without looking up from his book for more than a second), "Yes. A nine-banded armadillo. Did you know they always have four babies? Identical quadruplets—all girls or all boys—and if there's a bad drought the mama armadillo can stay pregnant as long as she needs to until it rains."

How did he know these things?!?

People with environmental intelligence have an intuitive connection to nature and a natural interest in all things natural. Like the mathematicians, they see patterns and enjoy classifying data. They see God's hand in the world around them, and it fascinates them. They also have a "way" with animals. They're "horse whisperers"...and dog whisperers, and cat whisperers, and lizard whisperers. We ran a veritable zoo for several years, and our menagerie always wagged, purred, or chirped when they were with this particular child because he pretty much "spoke their language" —our own Dr. Doolittle.

If you have an environmental "genius" at your house, pets sort of come with the package. You will also need to accommodate their inevitable collections of nature specimens. In addition, consider these suggestions as skill-builders:

Provide them with illustrated nature books and let them absorb data and trivia to their heart's content.

Consider subscriptions to nature magazines such as National Geographic Jr. or Ranger Rick.

Plan field trips to a natural history museum. Many host visiting exhibits, so you can go often for shorter stints.

Help them set up a weather station and/or build their own weather tracking equipment. Groups such as the National Oceanic and Atmospheric Association (NOAA) may fascinate them.

As often as possible, take advantage of opportunities to camp, hike, hunt, spelunk, snorkel, scuba...anything to get them outdoors and into nature!

Notes to Self

Summary

Each of us—and each of our children—are "fearfully and wonderfully made" (Psalm 139:14). We are a marvelously unique combination of perceptions, temperaments, learning styles, and creative gifts.

Finding the right key is not always easy, but the Bible tells us that if any man lacks wisdom, he should ask God, who gives to all men freely and without reproach. (James 1:5)

Keep knocking, and the doors will open!

Other Books in this Series

How to Make Learning Meaningful, Memorable and Fun!
(Book 2 – ebook, paperback, and online course available)

How to Encourage Creative Thinking
(Book 3 – ebook, paperback, and online course available)

How to Raise a Hero
(Book 4 – ebook, paperback and online course available)

The Homeschool Parents' How-To Handbook
Look for bundles that include all titles

Other Educational Works by this Author

Discover Texas

A hands-on, unit study-based history program to help families discover Texas, one adventure after another!

Other Books by this Author

More Precious Than Gold

The bullet that killed Eliza Gentry's fiancé shattered her dreams as well. Clinging to her battered faith, she heads west to escape her grief and runs headlong into the man who caused it.

Tall and headstrong, Eliza expects to remain an "unclaimed treasure." Devastated in the wake of the Civil War, she leaves her home in Texas and sets out for New Mexico's Sangre de Cristo mountains in search of peace and new purpose but discovers a wild western frontier where former enemies—Yankees and Rebels, Freedmen and Indians— square off in the quest for land and gold.

Eliza must confront her prejudices and fears, and Jacob Craig embodies that conflict. The mountain man wins her trust with his gentle strength, but he harbors a secret. As a Union sharp-shooter, he met her fiancé on the field of battle and cost him his life. Can she forgive him? To find peace and the future she yearns for, Eliza must first find in God a faith more precious than gold.

A real ghost town comes to life in this award-winning story of love, forgiveness, and the sovereignty of God. Christian historical fiction readers will love the way this story combines the adventure of classic historical western fiction with a dash of romance.

Home Sweet Hole: A Folio of "Feasible Fantasy" Floor Plans

"In a hole in the ground there lived a Hobbit..." but Hobbits aren't the only ones with down-to-earth dreams. This folio of "feasible fantasy" floor plans gives you a fun-loving peek inside a dozen earth-bermed dwellings in an imaginary borough of burrows—all drawn to scale as if the builder, himself, were offering an open house tour.

www.ingramcontent.com/pod-product-compliance
Lightning Source LLC
Chambersburg PA
CBHW071423040426
42445CB00012BA/1273